미순쌤의

초등
1~2학년
영어

방과 후
놀이 영어
수업 교재

미순쌤의
초등
1~2학년
영어

생각나눔

이 미 순 *Misoon Lee*

미국 Andrews University 졸업(석사)

홍연초, 녹천초, 경수초, 신남초, 구산초, 북성초, 개웅초, 경일초, 신정초, 방화초, 대청초, 청덕초 그 외 다수 방과 후 영어 강사

본 저자는 1995년에 한 초등학교에서 특기 적성 영어 강사로 강의를 시작한 이래로 다수의 초등학교와 중학교 그리고 고등학교에서 방과 후 영어 강사로 근무하였으며 현재도 활발하게 활동하는 중이다.

ALPHABET 대문자 및 소문자

자음: Consonant 모음: Vowel

A	-	a	N	-	n
B	-	b	O	-	o
C	-	c	P	-	p
D	-	d	Q	-	q
E	-	e	R	-	r
F	-	f	S	-	s
G	-	g	T	-	t
H	-	h	U	-	u
I	-	i	V	-	v
J	-	j	W	-	w
K	-	k	X	-	x
L	-	l	Y	-	y
M	-	m	Z	-	z

ABC

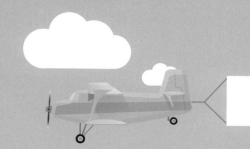

PREFACE

초등학교 1~2학년 영어가 부활하고 놀이 영어 방식과 음성 언어로 가르쳐야 한다는 교육청 지침이 나옴에 따라 기존 영어 강사들의 수업 운영 방식에 많은 변화가 생겼다. 그동안 놀이 영어 중심의 초등학교 1~2학년 방과 후 영어 교재로 마땅한 교재가 없어서 오랜 고민 끝에 이 책을 집필하게 되었다. 1995년에 특기 적성 영어 강사로 한 초등학교에서 강의를 한 이래로 수많은 경험과 노하우를 쌓으며 학생들을 가르쳐 왔고 미국에서 석사 학위를 위해 유학할 때 만난 수많은 외국 친구들에게 배운 미국의 문화와 언어가 내게 많은 도움이 되었다.

이 책은 알파벳 순서에 따라 1장 A에서 26장 Z에 이르기까지 다양한 내용을 담고 있다. 영어 단어, 영어 게임, 파닉스, 우주 이야기, 미국의 문화 등을 알기 쉽게 설명하였고 각 Chapter에 나오는 연관성 있는 것들로 색칠함으로써 다시 한 번 복습할 수 있도록 하였다. 또한, 미순 쌤의 기초 영어 회화를 통하여 배운 내용을 문장으로 말하는 연습을 하도록 하였다.

이 책으로 공부하는 모든 초등학교 1~2학년 학생들이 영어에 더욱 흥미와 관심을 갖고 열심히 공부함으로써 많은 발전이 있기를 소망하며 지도하시는 영어 선생님들께도 좋은 결과가 있기를 소망합니다.

이 미 순 *Misoon Lee*

이 책의 활용법

많은 초등학교 방과 후 수업은 3개월 단위로 수업이 진행되므로 일주일에 두 번 수업을 할 때 총 12주로 24번 수업을 하게 됩니다. 이 책은 총 26장으로 알파벳 순서로 기록되어 있는데 이 중 7장 Games와 24장 X-mas를 제외하고 수업마다 한 Chapter씩 수업을 하시면 됩니다. 7장은 game에 관해 자세히 설명했고 24장은 크리스마스 캐럴로 이루어져 있습니다. 또한, 부록에도 영어 노래가 몇 곡 있습니다. 매 수업 적절히 영어 노래와 영어 게임을 활용하시면 됩니다. Chapter마다 POWERPOINT를 사용하여 시각적 효과를 극대화하고, 또한 다양한 카드와 교구를 사용하셔서 수업에 생동감과 흥미를 주시고 제가 YouTube에 올리는 수업을 참고하시기 바랍니다.

YouTube로 들어가셔서 미순 쌤의 초등 1~2학년 영어를 검색하시기 바랍니다.

CONTENTS

Chapter 01

Animals

A	ant (개미)	N	nightingale (나이팅게일: 새 이름)
B	bat (박쥐)	O	otter (수달)
C	cat (고양이)	P	polar bear (북극곰)
D	dog (개)	Q	quail (메추라기)
E	elephant (코끼리)	R	rabbit (토끼)
F	fish (물고기)	S	sheep (양)
G	goose (거위)	T	turtle (바다거북)
H	hedgehog (고슴도치)	U	urial (우리알 산양: 야생의 양)
I	iguana (이구아나)	V	vulture (독수리)
J	jaguar (재규어)	W	whale (고래)
K	koala (코알라)	X	x-ray fish (투명어: 프리스텔라)
L	lizard (도마뱀)	Y	yak (야크)
M	mouse (쥐)	Z	zebra (얼룩말)

Other animals

alpaca (알파카)　　　bird (새)　　　crab (게)

deer (사슴)　　　duck (오리)　　　eagle (수리)

fox (여우)　　　frog (개구리)　　　giraffe (기린)

goat (염소)　　　gorilla (고릴라)　　　horse (말)

jackal (자칼)　　　kangaroo (캥거루)　　　lion (사자)

meerkat (미어캣)　　　monkey (원숭이)　　　octopus (문어)

penguin (펭귄)　　　prairie dog (프레리도그)　　　puma (퓨마)

raccoon (아메리카 너구리)　　　sea lion (바다사자)　　　snake (뱀)

tiger (호랑이)　　　walrus (바다코끼리)　　　wolf (늑대)

미순 쌤의
기초 영어 회화

A: What's your favorite animal?

B: It's a zebra.

Body

Body (신체)	**Arm** (팔)
Face (얼굴)	**Hand** (손)
Hair (머리카락)	**Foot** (발)
Head (머리)	**Neck** (목)
Forehead (이마)	**Shoulder** (어깨)
Eye (눈)	**Knee** (무릎)
Nose (코)	**Toe** (발가락)
Mouth (입)	**Leg** (다리)
Ear (귀)	**Nail** (손톱)
Lip (입술)	**Elbow** (팔꿈치)
Tongue (혀)	**Chin** (턱)
Finger (손가락)	**Cheek** (뺨)

미순 쌤의
기초 영어 회화

A: Look at those shapes. Aren't they cool?

B: Wow! Wonderful!

Countries

Republic of Korea (South Korea 대한민국)	**U.S.A.** (United States of America 미국)
U.K. (United Kingdom 영국)	**Canada** (캐나다)
Brazil (브라질)	**Denmark** (덴마크)
Norway (노르웨이)	**Sweden** (스웨덴)
Russia (러시아)	**Greece** (그리스)
Belgium (벨기에)	**France** (프랑스)
Italy (이탈리아)	**Spain** (스페인)
Germany (독일)	**Egypt** (이집트)
Australia (호주)	**Switzerland** (스위스)
Turkey (터키)	**India** (인도)
Vietnam (베트남)	**Taiwan** (대만)
China (중국)	**Japan** (일본)

미순 쌤의
기초 영어 회화

A: Where are you from?

B: I'm from South Korea.

Day & Night

Sun

The sun is the center of Earth's solar system. The sun is a star. It is the closest star to Earth, the planet you live on. The sun is very hot.

(해석) 태양은 지구의 태양계의 중심이다. 태양은 별이다. 그것은 당신이 살고 있는 행성인 지구와 가장 가까운 별이다. 태양은 매우 뜨겁다.

Moon

When you look into the sky at night, you can see Earth's moon. The moon orbits Earth, just like Earth orbits the sun.

(해석) 당신이 밤에 하늘을 볼 때, 당신은 지구의 달을 볼 수 있다. 달은 지구를 도는데, 지구가 태양을 도는 것과 같다.

Earth

Earth is a special planet. It is the only place we know of where there is life – plants and animals, including people. Earth is our home. Most of Earth is covered by oceans.

(해석) 지구는 특별한 행성이다. 그것은 생명이 있는 우리가 아는 유일한 장소이다.
- 식물과 동물, 사람을 포함한다. 지구는 우리의 집이다. 지구의 대부분은 대양으로 덮여 있다.

미순 쌤의
기초 영어 회화

A: Is the sun hot?

B: Yes, it is.

Emotion

hot (더운)

cold (추운)

hungry (배고픈)

thirsty (목마른)

happy (행복한)

sad (슬픈)

tired (피곤한)

angry (화난)

scared (무서운)

brave (용감한)

nervous (긴장되는, 불안한, 초조한)

excited (흥분한)

mad (화난)

worried (걱정되는)

surprised (놀란)

thankful (감사하는)

embarrassed (당황한)

lonely (외로운)

hopeful (희망적인)

silly (어리석은)

proud (자랑스러운, 당당한)

bored (지루한)

미순 쌤의
기초 영어 회화

A: How do you feel today?

B: I'm happy.

Family

family (가족)	**uncle** (아저씨, 삼촌)
relative (친척)	**aunt** (아주머니, 이모, 숙모)
dad (아빠)	**cousin** (사촌)
mom (엄마)	**husband** (남편)
sibling (남녀의 구별없이 형제 자매)	**wife** (아내)
brother (남자 형제)	**father-in-law** (시아버지, 장인)
sister (여자 형제)	**mother-in-law** (시어머니, 장모)
grandpa (할아버지)	**brother-in-law** (처남, 아주버님)
grandma (할머니)	**sister-in-law** (시누이, 올케)

*가계도를 family tree라고 한다.

미순 쌤의
기초 영어 회화

A: How many family members do you have?

B: I have four members. My mom, my dad,
   my sister and me.

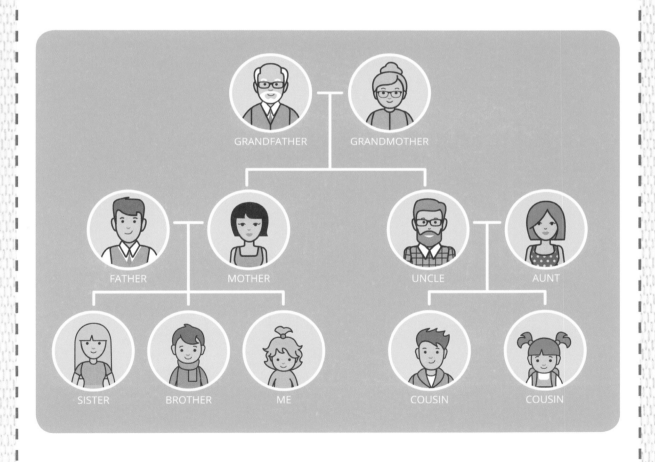

Games

Simon says(가라사대 게임)

ex) "Simon says stand up."이라고 했을 경우 학생들이 일어나야 하고, 만약 그냥 "Stand up."이라고 했을 때는 일어나면 안 됨. 마지막까지 남는 사람에게 상품 수여함

Mimic game(흉내 내기 게임)

ex) Mimic dog sound - 학생들은 woof나 bow wow라고 한다. Mimic cat sound - 학생들은 meow라고 한다. 가장 흉내를 잘 낸 학생에게 상품 수여함

Treasure hunt(보물찾기 게임)

보물 쪽지를 교실 안에 감추어 두고 찾는 학생에게는 상품을 준다.

Tic Tac Toe

우리나라의 오목과 비슷한 게임으로 O, X를 세 개 연달아 하면 이기는 게임
ex) X가 이긴 경우

		×
○	×	○
×	○	

UP & DOWN game

선생님이 숫자를 하나 생각한 후 학생들이 맞추게 하는 게임으로써 힌트를 up과 down을 사용하여 준다.
ex) 15가 정답인 경우 학생이 13이라고 하면 up이라고 말하고 17이라고 하면 down이라고 말한다. 숫자를 맞추는 학생에게 상품 수여함

동물 이름 영어로 맞히기 게임

동물의 특성을 설명해 주고 그 동물이 무엇인지를 영어로 맞추는 게임
ex) 다리와 목이 유난히 긴 동물로 육상 포유류 중 키가 가장 큰 동물
(정답: giraffe - 기린)

과일 이름 영어로 맞히기 게임

과일의 특성을 설명해 주고 그 과일이 무엇인지를 영어로 맞추는 게임
ex) 노랗고 긴 모양이며 부드럽고 맛이 좋은 과일
(정답: banana - 바나나)

미순 쌤의
기초 영어 회화

A: Can you play a game with me?

B: Yes, I can.

Meow

Woof

Holidays & House

Holidays(휴일)

Memorial Day (현충일)   Mother's Day (어머니의 날)

Christmas (성탄절)   Labor Day (노동절)

Thanksgiving Day (추수감사절)   Valentine's Day (발렌타인 데이)

Easter (부활절)   April Fool's Day (만우절)

Halloween (할로윈)   New Year's Day (설날)

Independence Day (독립 기념일)   Veterans Day (재향 군인의 날)

House(집)

attic (다락)   living room (거실)

bedroom (침실)   dining room (식당)

bathroom (욕실)   garage (차고)

kitchen (부엌)   yard (마당, 뜰)

미순 쌤의
기초 영어 회화

A: Have you ever taken an elephant train?

B: Yes, I have.

Chapter 09

Instruments

piano (피아노)

violin (바이올린)

cello (첼로)

viola (비올라)

double bass (더블 베이스)

guitar (기타)

drum (드럼, 북)

pipe organ (파이프 오르간)

harp (하프)

trumpet (트럼펫)

tuba (튜바)

keyboard (키보드)

cymbals (심벌즈)

xylophone (실로폰)

flute (플루트)

clarinet (클라리넷)

saxophone (색소폰)

recorder (리코더)

harmonica (하모니카)

tambourine (탬버린)

*악기를 연주하다는 표현을 쓸 때
play the piano(피아노를 연주하다)
play the guitar(기타를 연주하다)
play the harp(하프를 연주하다)

미순 쌤의
기초 영어 회화

A: Which instrument can you play?

B: I can play the piano.

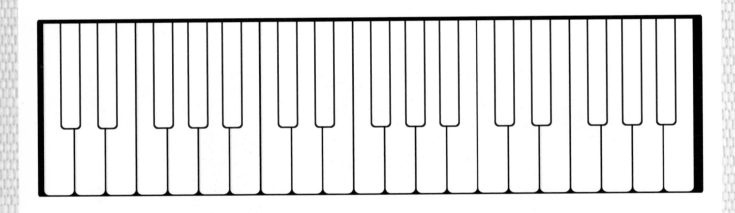

Jobs

mechanic (자동차 수리공)

barber (이발사)

lifeguard (인명 구조원)

lawyer (변호사)

actor (배우/남자)

writer (작가)

cook (요리사)

waiter (웨이터/남자)

nurse (간호사)

doctor (의사)

police officer (경찰관)

farmer (농부)

zookeeper (사육사)

dentist (치과의사)

banker (은행가)

engineer (기술자)

judge (판사)

vet (수의사)

plumber (배관공)

teacher (선생님)

student (학생)

pilot (비행기 조종사)

fire fighter (소방관)

pastor (목사님)

미순 쌤의
기초 영어 회화

A: What do you do?

B: I'm a teacher.

Chapter 11 Kid's vocabulary

7 days of the week(요일)

Sunday (일요일)	**Monday** (월요일)	**Tuesday** (화요일)
Wednesday (수요일)	**Thursday** (목요일)	**Friday** (금요일)
Saturday (토요일)		

12 months(12달)

January (1월)	**February** (2월)	**March** (3월)
April (4월)	**May** (5월)	**June** (6월)
July (7월)	**August** (8월)	**September** (9월)
October (10월)	**November** (11월)	**December** (12월)

Season(계절)

spring (봄)	**summer** (여름)	**fall or autumn** (가을)	**winter** (겨울)

Kinds of Vehicles(운송 수단의 종류)

ship (배)	**car** (자동차)	**truck** (트럭)
bicycle (자전거)	**motorcycle** (오토바이)	**helicopter** (헬리콥터)
airplane (비행기)	**bus** (버스)	**train** (기차)
subway (지하철)	**carriage** (마차)	**tram** (전차)
boat (보트)	**taxi** (택시)	**ambulance** (구급차)
cab (택시)	**van** (밴)	**scooter** (스쿠터)

미순 쌤의
기초 영어 회화

A: Do you take a subway when you go to work?

B: Yes, I do.

01

2020 JANUARY

Sun	Mon	Tue	Wed	Thu	Fri	Sat
			1	2	3	4
5	6	7	8	9	10	11
12	13	14	15	16	17	18
19	20	21	22	23	24	25
26	27	28	29	30	31	

Long vowels

mouse [maus]   loud [laud]
ou가 '아우' 발음이 난다.

soup [su:p]   you [ju:]
ou가 '우~' 발음이 난다.

cake [keik]   snake [sneik]
a_e가 '에이' 발음이 난다.

tiger [taigər]   fire [faiər]
i가 '아이' 발음이 난다.

nose [nouz]   stone [stoun]
o_e가 '오우' 발음이 난다.

cube [kju:b]   flute [flu:t]
u_e가 '우~' 발음이 난다.

green [gri:n]   tree [tri:]
ee가 '이~' 발음이 난다.

미순 쌤의
기초 영어 회화

A: What are vowels?

B: A, E, I, O, U.

AEIOU

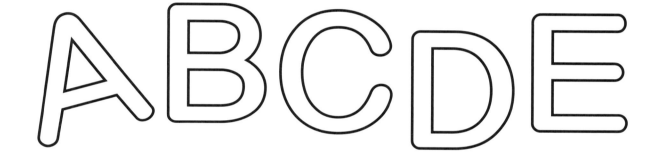

Math

Math (수학)

+	plus (더하기)	÷	divided by (나누기)
−	minus (빼기)	=	equal (같은, 같음)
×	times (곱하기)		

ex)

$2 + 3 = 5$ addition (덧셈)

$7 - 3 = 4$ subtraction (뺄셈)

$3 × 5 = 15$ multiplication (곱셈)

$20 ÷ 5 = 4$ division (나눗셈)

Calculation (계산)

$3 + 4 =$

$2 + 7 =$

$10 - 5 =$

$20 - 12 =$

$7 × 9 =$

$2 × 8 =$

$12 ÷ 4 =$

$15 ÷ 5 =$

미순 쌤의
기초 영어 회화

A: What is your favorite subject?

B: It's math.

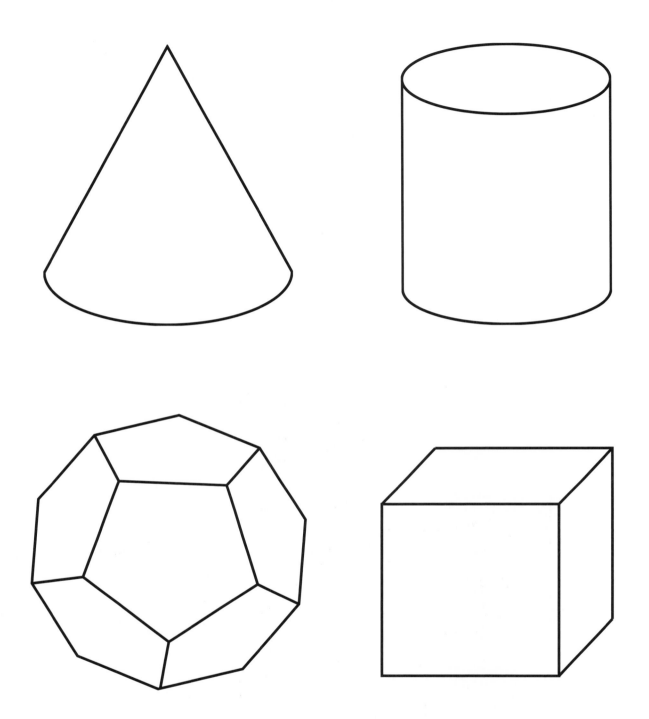

Numbers

1	one	11	eleven
2	two	12	twelve
3	three	13	thirteen
4	four	14	fourteen
5	five	15	fifteen
6	six	16	sixteen
7	seven	17	seventeen
8	eight	18	eighteen
9	nine	19	nineteen
10	ten	20	twenty

짝수 – an even number

홀수 – an odd number

미순 쌤의
기초 영어 회화

A: Tell me two even numbers.

B: Two & six.

Chapter 15 · Official language

English (영어)

1. U.S.A. (미국)
2. U.K. (영국)
3. Canada (캐나다)
4. Australia (호주)
5. Singapore (싱가포르)

Spanish (스페인어)

1. Spain (스페인)
2. Mexico (멕시코)
3. Peru (페루)
4. Argentina (아르헨티나)

Portuguese (포르투갈어)

1. Portugal (포르투갈)
2. Brazil (브라질)
3. Angola (앙골라)

French (프랑스어)

1. France (프랑스)
2. Monaco (모나코)
3. Senegal (세네갈)

German (독일어)

1. Germany (독일)
2. Austria (오스트리아)
3. Switzerland (스위스)

*Official language of countries (공식 언어)

미순 쌤의
기초 영어 회화

A: What language do you speak in South Korea?

B: We speak Korean.

How are you?
Fine. Thanks.

Places

Places(장소들)

airport (공항)

apartment (아파트)

bakery (빵집)

bank (은행)

beauty salon (미용실)

church (교회)

company (회사)

dental clinic (치과)

fire station (소방서)

gas station (주유소)

hospital (병원)

house (집)

laundry (세탁소)

park (공원)

pharmacy (약국)

police station (경찰서)

post office (우체국)

restaurant (음식점)

school (학교)

shopping mall (백화점, 쇼핑몰)

store (가게)

zoo (동물원)

미순 쌤의
기초 영어 회화

A: How often do you go to post office?

B: I go there once a month.

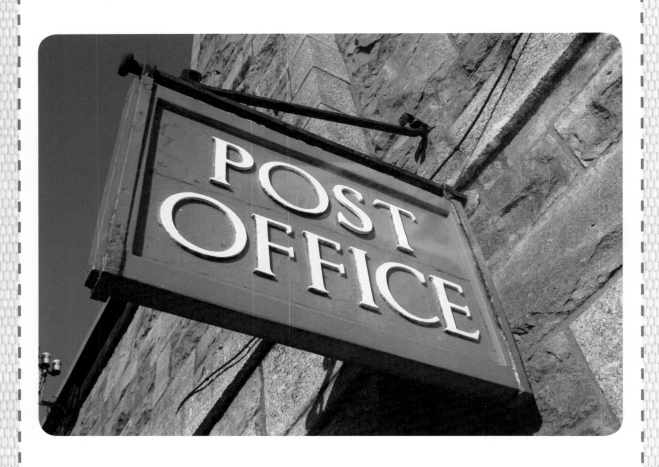

Quiz

Q: Who is the first President of the U.S.A?

A: George Washington

Q: What is the capital of the U.S.A?

A: Washington, D.C.

Q: How many states does the U.S.A. have?

A: 50

Q: What do people in the U.S.A. eat on Thanksgiving Day?

A: Turkey, pumpkin pie

Q: When children visit someone's house on Halloween, what do they say?

A: Trick or treat

Q: When is Christmas?

A: December 25th.

Q: When is Independence Day in the U.S.A?

A: July 4th.

Q: What do people call the President's house in the U.S.A?

A: The White House

Q: Who is the first person to travel to the moon?

A: Neil Armstrong

미순 쌤의
기초 영어 회화

A: What do you eat on New Year's day in South Korea?

B: We eat tteokguk.

Rainbow colors

Rainbow colors

Red　　　(빨간색)
Orange　(주황색)
Yellow　(노란색)
Green　　(초록색)
Blue　　 (파란색)
Indigo　 (남색)
Purple　 (보라색)

Other colors

Pink　　 (분홍색)
Black　　(검은색)
White　　(흰색)
Gold　　 (금색)
Silver　 (은색)
Brown　 (갈색)
Gray　　 (회색)

Mixing colors

blue + yellow = green
blue + white = light blue
red + yellow = orange
blue + black = dark blue

미순 쌤의
기초 영어 회화

A: What is your favorite color?

B: It's red.

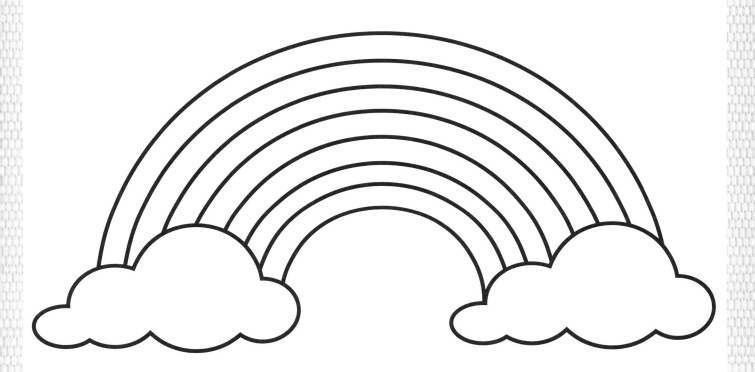

Chapter 19 Shapes & Schools

Shapes(모양)

circle (원)	semi-circle (반원)	oval (타원형)
triangle (삼각형)	square (정사각형)	rectangle (직사각형)
diamond (마름모)	arch (아치)	cone (원뿔)
heart (하트)	crescent (초승달)	star (별)

Schools(학교)

preschool (어린이집)	kindergarten (유치원)
elementary school (초등학교)	middle school (중학교)
high school (고등학교)	college (단과대학)
university (종합대학)	graduate school (대학원)

미순 쌤의
기초 영어 회화

A: What elementary school do you attend?

B: Changdong elementary school.

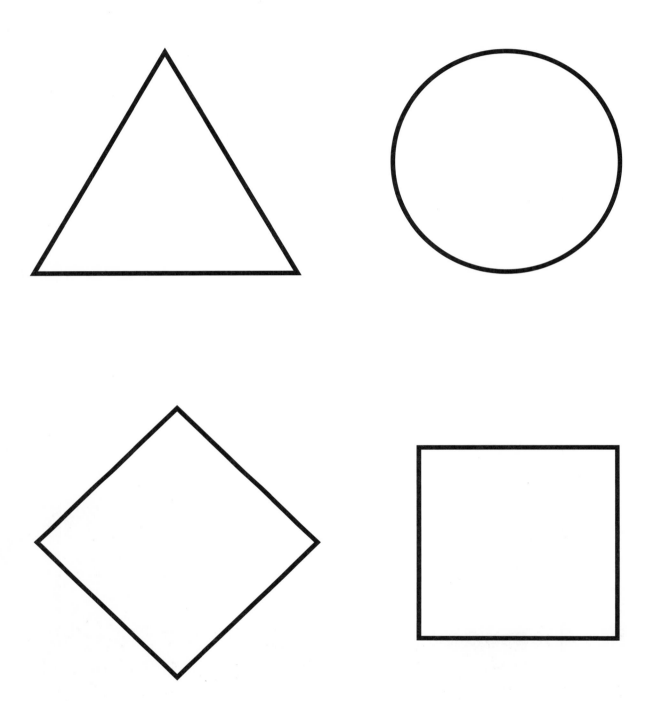

Chapter 20

Time & Trip

What time is it? (몇 시 입니까?)

3:00
It is three o'clock. (3시입니다.)

3:15
It is three fifteen. (3시 15분입니다.)

3:30
It is three thirty. (3시 30분입니다.)

3:45
It is three forty-five. (3시 45분입니다.)

Trip to U.S.A. (미국으로의 여행)

passport (여권)
visa (비자)
airplane ticket (비행기 표)
money (돈)

미순 쌤의
기초 영어 회화

A: How much is it?

B: It's ten dollars.

Chapter 21

Universe

Universe (우주)	Solar system (태양계)
Sun (태양)	Moon (달)
Star (별)	Planet (행성)
Mercury (수성)	Venus (금성)
Earth (지구)	Mars (화성)
Jupiter (목성)	Saturn (토성)
Uranus (천왕성)	Neptune (해왕성)
Pluto (명왕성)	Galaxy (은하)
Comet (혜성)	Black holes (블랙홀)
Meteor (유성)	Meteorite (운석)
Spaceship (우주선)	Telescope (망원경)

8 planets in our solar system

Planet (행성)	별의 궤도를 도는 우주 안에 있는 크고 동그란 물체
Mercury (수성)	태양계 안의 8개의 행성들 중 가장 작은 행성
Venus (금성)	지구와 가장 가깝고 태양계 안에서 가장 뜨거운 행성
Earth (지구)	지구는 식물과 동물이 있고 사람이 사는 특별한 행성
Mars (화성)	지구의 하루와 화성의 하루는 거의 같음
Jupiter (목성)	태양계 안의 8개의 행성들 중 가장 큰 행성
Saturn (토성)	수천 개의 ring을 가지고 있는 행성
Uranus (천왕성)	태양계 안의 8개의 행성들 중 가장 추운 행성
Neptune (해왕성)	태양으로부터 가장 멀리 떨어져 있는 행성

미순 쌤의
기초 영어 회화

A: What is the biggest planet in our solar system?

B: It's Jupiter.

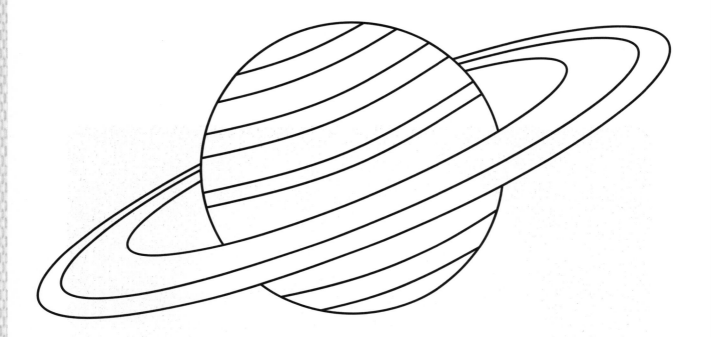

Vegetables & Fruits

Vegetables(채소)

tomato (토마토)	mushroom (버섯)	turnip (순무)
lettuce (상추)	garlic (마늘)	onion (양파)
green onion (파: 소파)	carrot (당근)	celery (셀러리)
cabbage (양배추)	spinach (시금치)	chilli pepper (칠리 고추)
cucumber (오이)	potato (감자)	sweet potato (고구마)
radish (무)	eggplant (가지)	corn (옥수수)
broccoli (브로콜리)	ginger (생강)	peas (완두콩)
pumpkin (호박)	kale (케일)	asparagus (아스파라거스)

Fruits(과일)

fig (무화과)	apple (사과)	banana (바나나)
orange (오렌지)	grapes (포도)	watermelon (수박)
melon (메론)	pineapple (파인애플)	pear (배)
cherry (체리)	plum (자두)	lemon (레몬)
strawberry (딸기)	peach (복숭아)	mango (망고)
grapefruit (자몽)	lime (라임)	blueberry (블루베리)
avocado (아보카도)	chestnut (밤)	persimmon (감)
tangerine (귤)	pomegranate (석류)	kiwi (키위)

미순 쌤의
기초 영어 회화

A: What's your favorite fruit?

B: It's a mango.

Weather

Weather(날씨)

sunny (맑은)	**cloudy** (구름이 있는)
windy (바람이 부는)	**foggy** (안개가 낀)
hot (더운)	**cold** (추운)
cool (시원한)	**rainy** (비 오는)
snowy (눈 오는)	**stormy** (폭풍의)
wet (습한)	**dry** (건조한)

날씨가 어때요?
How is the weather?
= What is the weather like?

바람이 불어요.
It is windy.

미순 쌤의
기초 영어 회화

A: How is the weather?

B: It's sunny.

X-mas

Christmas songs

Santa Claus is coming to town

You'd better watch out! You'd better not cry
Better not pout, I'm telling you why
Santa Claus is coming to town
He's making a list, and checking it twice;
gonna find out who's naughty or nice
Santa Claus is coming to town
He sees you when you're sleeping
he knows when you're awake
He knows if you've been bad or good
so be good for goodness sake! Ohhh. . .
You'd better watch out! You'd better not cry
Better not pout, I'm telling you why
Santa Claus is coming to town
He sees you when you're sleeping
he knows when you're awake
He knows if you've been bad or good
so be good for goodness sake! Ohhh. . .
You'd better watch out! You'd better not cry
Better not pout, I'm telling you why
Santa Claus is coming to town

We wish you a Merry Christmas

We wish you a Merry Christmas
We wish you a Merry Christmas
We wish you a Merry Christmas
And a happy New Year!
Good tidings we bring to you and your kin
We wish you a Merry Christmas
And a happy New Year!
Oh, bring us some figgy pudding
Oh, bring us some figgy pudding
Oh, bring us some figgy pudding
And bring it right here
We won't go until we get some
We won't go until we get some
We won't go until we get some
So bring it right here
We all like our figgy pudding
We all like our figgy pudding
We all like our figgy pudding
With all its good cheer!
We wish you a Merry Christmas
We wish you a Merry Christmas
We wish you a Merry Christmas
And a happy New Year!

미순 쌤의
기초 영어 회화

A: How was your last Christmas?

B: It was great.

Yes or No

Q: **Are you a teacher?** (당신은 선생님입니까?)
A: Yes, I am. (네, 그렇습니다.)
A: No, I'm not. (아니오, 그렇지 않습니다.)

Q: **Do you like ice cream?** (당신은 아이스크림을 좋아합니까?)
A: Yes, I do. (네, 그렇습니다.)
A: No, I don't. (아니오, 그렇지 않습니다.)

Q: **Can you swim?** (당신은 수영을 할 수 있습니까?)
A: Yes, I can. (네, 할 수 있습니다.)
A: No, I can't. (아니오, 할 수 없습니다.)

Q: **May I sit down here?** (내가 여기에 앉아도 될까요?)
A: Yes, you may. (네, 앉아도 됩니다.)
A: No, you may not. (아니오, 앉으면 안 됩니다.)

Q: **Don't you like apples?** (너 사과 좋아하지 않니?)
A: Yes, I do. ('네, 좋아해요.' 라는 의미)
A: No, I don't. ('아니오, 좋아하지 않아요.' 라는 의미)

한국말과는 달리 영어에서는 긍정으로 질문하든, 부정으로 질문하든 상관없이 Yes는 질문하는 동사의 의미로 그렇다는 뜻이고, No는 그렇지 않다는 뜻입니다. 이 점 유의하시기 바랍니다.

미순 쌤의
기초 영어 회화

A: Don't you like fish?

B: No, I don't.

Zoo animals

Zoo animals(동물원 동물들)

monkey (원숭이)	elephant (코끼리)	kangaroo (캥거루)
snake (뱀)	bear (곰)	giraffe (기린)
zebra (얼룩말)	lion (사자)	tiger (호랑이)
parrot (앵무새)	crocodile (악어)	alligator (악어)
hippo (하마)	horse (말)	lizard (도마뱀)
goat (염소)	donkey (당나귀)	deer (사슴)
alpaca (알파카)	jaguar (재규어)	leopard (표범)
fox (여우)	hyena (하이에나)	flamingo (홍학)

Aquarium(수족관)

dolphin (돌고래)	whale (고래)	penguin (펭귄)
seal (물범)	shark (상어)	sea lion (바다사자)
otter (수달)	seahorse (해마)	starfish (불가사리)
jellyfish (해파리)	frog (개구리)	turtle (거북)
tortoise (땅거북)	crocodile (악어)	octopus (문어)
ray (가오리)	crab (게)	shrimp (새우)
lobster (바닷가재)	squid (오징어)	snail (달팽이)

미순 쌤의
기초 영어 회화

A: What is the king of sea?

B: It's a shark.

English songs

Deep and wide

Deep and wide deep and wide
There's a fountain flowing deep and wide
Deep and wide deep and wide
There's a fountain flowing deep and wide

BINGO

There was a farmer had a dog and Bingo was his name O
BINGO BINGO BINGO and Bingo was his name O

Twinkle twinkle little star

Twinkle twinkle little star How I wonder what you are
Up above the world so high Like a diamond in the sky
Twinkle twinkle little star How I wonder what you are

Ten little kids

One little two little three little kids four little five little six
little kids seven little eight little nine little kids ten little
kids

Head shoulders knees and toes

Head shoulders knees and toes knees and toes
Head shoulders knees and toes knees and toes
Eyes and ears and mouth and nose
Head shoulders knees and toes knees and toes

Finger family

Daddy finger daddy finger where are you?
Here I am here I am how do you do?
Mommy finger mommy finger where are you?
Here I am here I am how do you do?
Brother finger brother finger where are you?
Here I am here I am how do you do?
Sister finger sister finger where are you?
Here I am here I am how do you do?
Baby finger baby finger where are you?
Here I am here I am how do you do?

Edelweiss

Edelweiss Edelweiss Every morning you greet me
Small and white clean and bright
You look happy to meet me
Blossom of snow may you bloom and grow
bloom and grow forever
Edelweiss Edelweiss Bless my homeland forever

Happy happy home

With daddy in the family happy happy home
happy happy home happy happy home
With daddy in the family happy happy home
happy happy home

Do Re Mi song

Doe – a deer a female deer
Ray – a drop of golden sun
Me – a name I call myself
Far – a long long way to run
Sew – a needle pulling thread
La – a note to follow sew
Tea – a drink with jam and bread
That will bring us back to doe
Doe ray me far sew la tea doe sew doe

If you're happy and you know it

If you're happy and you know it, clap your hands!
If you're happy and you know it, clap your hands!
If you're happy and you know it,
and you really want to show it,
If you're happy and you know it, clap your hands!

If you're happy and you know it, stamp your feet!
If you're happy and you know it, stamp your feet!
If you're happy and you know it,
and you really want to show it,
If you're happy and you know it, stamp your feet!

If you're happy and you know it, say "Ha Ha"!
If you're happy and you know it, say "Ha Ha"!
If you're happy and you know it,
and you really want to show it,
If you're happy and you know it, say "Ha Ha"!

미순쌤의

초등
1~2학년
영어

펴 낸 날 2020년 7월 27일

지 은 이 이미순
펴 낸 이 이기성
편집팀장 이윤숙
기획편집 정은지, 윤가영
표지디자인 정은지
책임마케팅 강보현, 류상만
펴 낸 곳 도서출판 생각나눔
출판등록 제 2018-000288호
주   소 서울 잔다리로7안길 22, 태성빌딩 3층
전   화 02-325-5100
팩   스 02-325-5101
홈페이지 www.생각나눔.kr
이 메 일 bookmain@think-book.com

• 책값은 표지 뒷면에 표기되어 있습니다.
  ISBN 979-11-7048-126-3 (63740)